EL 8/15

00038259   P

362.29B

WITHDRAWN
27/6/23
SM

Need to Know
Ecstasy

Sean Connolly

www.heinemann.co.uk
visit our website to find out more information about **Heinemann Library** books.

To order:
 Phone 44 (0) 1865 888066

Send a fax to 44 (0) 1865 314091

Visit the Heinemann Bookshop at www.heinemann.co.uk to browse our catalogue and order online.

First published in Great Britain by Heinemann Library, Halley Court, Jordan Hill, Oxford OX2 8EJ,
a division of Reed Educational and Professional Publishing Ltd.

Heinemann is a registered trademark of Reed Educational & Professional Publishing Limited.

Oxford Melbourne Auckland Johannesburg Blantyre Gaborone Ibadan Portsmouth NH (USA) Chicago

Designed by M2 Graphic Design
Printed in Hong Kong / China
Originated by Ambassador Litho Ltd.

04 03 02 01 00
10 9 8 7 6 5 4 3 2 1

ISBN 0431 09781X

British Library Cataloguing in Publication Data
Sean Connolly
Ecstasy – (Need to know)
1. MDMA (Drug) – Juvenile literature 2. MDMA (Drug) – Physiological effect – Juvenile literature
I. Title 362.2'94

Acknowledgements
The Publishers would like to thank the following for permission to reproduce photographs: Advertising
Archive: pg.49; Camera Press: pg.4, pg.10, pg.11, pg.17, pg.22, pg.38, pg.39; Format: pg.26, pg.29,
pg.50; Magnum Photos: pg.6, pg.8; Mary Evans Picture Library: pg.15; Pa Photos: pg.32, pg.36;
Photofusion: Mark Campbell pg.19; Retna: pg.12, pg.34, pg.35, pg.47; Rex Features: pg.5, pg.21,
pg.23, pg.25, pg.27, pg.31, pg.43, pg.45; Science Photo Library: pg.6, pg.30, pg.37; Telegraph
Colour Library: pg.41.

Cover photograph reproduced with permission of Science Photo Library.

Every effort has been made to contact copyright holders of any material reproduced in this book.
Any omissions will be rectified in subsequent printings if notice is given to the publisher.

Any words appearing in the text in bold, **like this**, are explained in the Glossary.

Contents

Introduction

Ecstasy is a drug that has been used widely for hardly more than a decade but during that time it has generated an enormous amount of publicity. Some people see it as a harmless element of a good time – something that helps make people feel happy and energetic enough to dance the night away. Other people see it as a worrying new addition to a drug pharmacy that is already bursting with ways of avoiding reality.

The controversy surrounding ecstasy is made worse because it has revived the idea of the 'generation gap' – the unbridgeable gulf between young people and their parents. Ecstasy represents something of an unknown for parents, since it has become popular in the period since their own teenage years. They cannot be sure whether any knowledge they might have about the dangers of other drugs – alcohol, cannabis and tobacco, for example – applies to ecstasy.

A way of life that includes taking ecstasy has grown in many holiday resorts fashionable with young people.

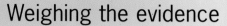

Weighing the evidence

In order for young people – and their parents – to understand ecstasy it is important to find some facts that can be used as evidence. It is also vital to accept that there are some things we just do not know, for example, about the lasting effects of repeated use. We can say, however, that ecstasy use has become widespread because those who take it usually enjoy the experience. Taking it does not make people violent or aggressive. However, there is mounting evidence that taking the drug itself can lead to death.

Despite its carefree reputation, people definitely *have* died after taking ecstasy, even in its pure form (as in the case of Leah Betts, see pages 32–33). Moreover, using ecstasy leads to a number of serious problems, most of which stem from the way it heats the body and encourages people to dance for hours – and some end up being taken away on a stretcher. Even more frightening is the lack of knowledge about how long-term use of ecstasy might harm people. These concerns themselves should make people think twice before calling ecstasy the 'happy drug'.

What is ecstasy?

Ecstasy, or 'E', is a drug that combines some of the effects of **hallucinogens** such as LSD with those of **stimulants** such as amphetamines. This combination of effects means that ecstasy distorts the user's outlook while at the same time seeming to provide them with the energy to go without sleep or food.

A large family

The chemical name for ecstasy is MDMA, which is short for methylene-dioxymethamphetamine. MDMA is just one of 179 members of a family of drugs known as MDA, which are derived from the oils of nutmeg, sassafras, saffron and crocus. Scientists are able to restructure the molecules of MDA elements to create this dramatic array of different drugs. Depending on how these molecules are arranged, the effects of the resulting drug vary from being very like amphetamines – which give the user confidence and a general boost – to being strongly hallucinogenic.

The effects

The initial effects of taking ecstasy begin about twenty minutes to an hour after the user swallows a pill. These effects are like those of amphetamines – the user feels more energetic and less inclined to feel hungry or tired. At the same time it raises the blood pressure, heart rate and body temperature. People often get a feeling like butterflies in the stomach and various tingling sensations.

These slightly nervous reactions soon fade and the user begins to feel happy and confident. This comfortable feeling can border on **euphoria**, coupled with a sense of serenity and closeness to those around. The effects peak at about two hours and wind slowly down for another two to four hours. Although ecstasy is sometimes described as being a mild hallucinogen, it is very rare for a user to hallucinate. Sometimes, though, users find a tendency to indulge in repetitive behaviour, such as shaking their head over and over. The setting – usually a loud dance floor – can encourage such impulses.

What is ecstasy?

The appeal of ecstasy

In some circles, ecstasy is called 'the love drug'. This reflects one of the main attractions of ecstasy – the way in which it seems linked to feeling good and a sense of shared purpose. Many ecstasy users still refer to being 'loved-up' when describing the effects of the drug.

The important thing about ecstasy – which provides another clue to its popularity – is that it is a drug that people prefer to take together. The term 'inclusiveness' is often heard when people describe ecstasy and there is a feeling that everyone in a large group is somehow part of a 'team'. The sense of well-being that the drug produces is enforced by the sight of dozens or even hundreds of others undergoing and sharing the same experience.

It is this feeling of togetherness and shared sensations that makes raves such popular venues for taking ecstasy. Whereas a similar number of people drinking alcohol could turn aggressive or violent, an ecstasy crowd is more likely to 'chill out' in the collective sense of affection. For this reason, women tend to feel less threatened in an ecstasy setting, and the fact is that the drug only rarely makes people feel sexier than usual.

The downside

As with LSD, whether the experience is good or bad depends on the user's frame of mind before taking the drug. An unsettled mood or a sense of anxiety about the surroundings can lead to a milder version of an LSD 'bad trip', where the user feels panicky and out of control. Weekend ecstasy users also report feeling down in the middle of the week.

The other negative effects of ecstasy include medical complications. There is mounting evidence that regular use might cause liver damage. The heart can be strained to the point of failure if blood pressure skyrockets. Most importantly, the **dehydration** associated with ecstasy can lead to **heat-stroke**, **respiratory** collapse and kidney failure.

The social mix

Although the very nature of the ecstasy 'high' is inclusive – in the sense that users tend not to be critical of each other – there are a few patterns that are immediately obvious. One of the most apparent is the overwhelming proportion of young users. Other drugs attract young people, but few are so closely linked to the young and to contemporary youth culture.

Weekend routine

Some of the statistics available underline ecstasy's popularity with the young. There are varying estimates of how many people take ecstasy each weekend, but the figures range between 500,000 and 800,000 in Britain alone. The UK's Institute for the Study of Drug **Dependence** (ISDD) has made a study of all available statistics relating to drug use among the young.

The study confirms that cannabis is by far the most popular illegal drug among young users, but that the most dramatic rise in drug use in the 1990s was the increase in 'dance drugs', especially ecstasy. The increase was especially pronounced among young people aged between sixteen and twenty-four.

'E' culture

While the typical ecstasy user has one or two tablets each weekend, there are a few settings that have become part of the 'E culture', as it is known. Ibiza, one of the Balearic Islands off the coast of Spain, is one of them. Its comforting summer warmth – extending long into the night – is ideal for an all-night rave. A whole way of life has evolved around the Ibiza rave scene, which – despite what some club-owners might say – depends on the reputation for ecstasy-friendly activities. Night after night of dancing reinforces the slightly skewed view of the world that is common with ecstasy. That view lingers long after clubbers have returned to their own country.

"Some 2.7 million ecstasy tablets, with a street value of £40.5 million, are sold in the UK every weekend. Seventeen-year-olds are averaging more than £100 a month to satisfy this habit..."

(Lord Sempill, speaking in the House of Lords, November 1996)

Ecstasy is commonly taken within a group setting, either on a crowded dance-floor with a powerful sound system, or in an outdoor 'tribal gathering'.

Is ecstasy addictive?

The word **addictive** triggers concern in many people, especially parents who think their children might be involved with ecstasy. It represents the ultimate danger of drug abuse, of being drawn into a spiral of increased use, craving, desperation and finally criminal activity and possible **overdose**.

Clearer definitions

Doctors and drug counsellors, however, prefer to use the term **dependence** when discussing the regular use of a drug. A number of different factors can contribute to either a physical or **psychological** dependence. Physical dependence is usually linked to the idea of **tolerance**, meaning that the body needs to have increasing amounts of a drug for it to have the same effect. The body begins to expect this increased amount and goes through **withdrawal** if supplies stop. Alcohol and heroin are good examples of drugs that promote physical dependence. Psychological dependence, as the name suggests, is to do with the mind's 'need' for the drug to cope with stress or difficult situations. Alcohol also produces a psychological dependence, as do cocaine and amphetamines.

Not quite the 'all clear'

Compared with these 'textbook examples', ecstasy emerges as a drug that does not promote dependence in regular users. It does, however, lead to a certain amount of tolerance. Although withdrawal cannot compare with the 'cold turkey' of heroin or alcohol, there are some symptoms of depression and anxiety that can emerge when people stop using ecstasy.

Some of these psychological reactions relate to what doctors call the 'rebound effect' of drugs, meaning that they eventually lead to sensations that are exactly opposite to those they first provided. Heroin, which offers a stress-free comfort blanket to first-time users, eventually leads to panic and near-desperation. Amphetamines, which are noted for supplying energy, can end up draining a user of all energy reserves. Ecstasy also produces a sense of anxiety, fatigue and depression in the person who once found care-free excitement and buzz.

The trance-like state that ecstasy induces – with a heightened sense of colours and sounds – causes some people to take the drug regularly.

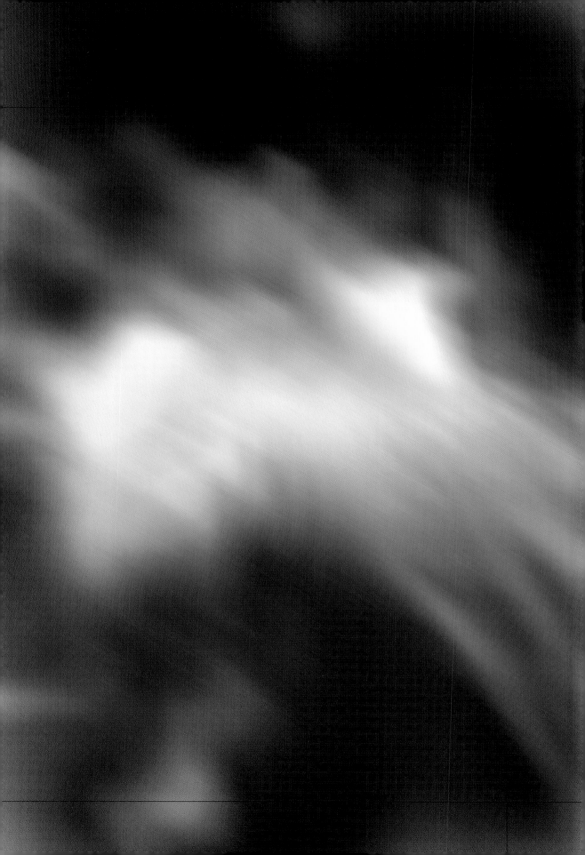

Ecstasy's history

Although it appears very much in the headlines nowadays, ecstasy has had a chequered history in the nine decades of its existence. It surfaces as a publicized drug, and then drifts back into relative obscurity. Its up-and-down history is partly due to the very mixture of effects that makes it so popular among ravers. It increases sensations of colour and sound but cannot be described as a true **hallucinogen** and it provides long-term energy without the sense of edginess associated with amphetamines.

German research

German **pharmacologists** at the beginning of the twentieth century were involved in intense research, to produce new drugs for the public. Many of today's drugs of abuse were developed at around that time, in the flurry of medical research. Cocaine, morphine and heroin were seen as 'medical breakthrough' drugs when these chemists developed them, towards the end of the nineteenth century. However, by the early 1900s their true effects were emerging.

LSD – developed in neighbouring Switzerland in the 1930s and 1940s – was also produced as a **therapeutic** drug. Such research was often very hit-or-miss. A basic drug would be isolated – usually from a natural source such as a plant – and then it would undergo a number of alterations as scientists tested for positive effects. Along the way some drugs were produced which were not intended to be used on their own, but were useful stepping stones in the production of other **pharmaceuticals**.

MDMA, which we now know as ecstasy, was one such stepping stone. It was first **synthesized** by chemists working for the Merck pharmaceutical company in Darmstadt, Germany, in 1912, and **patented** in 1914. Despite widespread stories nowadays that the drug was developed as an appetite **suppressant**, MDMA was simply a useful tool for producing other drugs. The upheavals of the **First World War** caused MDMA to be largely forgotten as chemists turned their attention to wartime efforts.

Fresh attempts

MDMA remained virtually unknown until 1939, when researchers began a series of tests to see if it would work as an appetite **suppressant** or as a **synthetic** version of adrenaline, the hormone that the body produces to deal with stress. Wartime activity – this time it was the **Second World War** – put an end to these tests, and it was only after the war that scientific reports about the drug began to appear in Polish scientific papers.

The post-war period ushered in the tense **Cold War** era, and the **intelligence** departments of many countries began experimenting with drugs to see if they could be used as weapons. One of the drugs that seemed promising in this area was LSD, and military scientists tried similar experiments with MDMA. Unlike LSD, which began to filter on to the streets because of its obvious power, MDMA once more faded into the background because it was less effective in research. The military also abandoned research on MDA – the more powerful 'parent drug' of MDMA.

The 'love drug'

In the 1960s a Californian chemist named Alexander Shulgin began **synthesizing** large quantities of **hallucinogens**, and spread the word about MDA and MDMA. Dubbed the 'love drug' by Californian drug takers, MDA was soon made illegal because its effects resembled those of LSD. In 1972, MDMA – ecstasy – entered the scene as a legal alternative.

California in the early 1970s provided fertile territory for the introduction of a legal drug that promised to make people feel happy, energetic and friendly towards each other. Marriage counsellors and therapists recommended 'ecstasy' – as it was now known – to the public. It seemed as though the drug provided a way of making people feel better about themselves while drawing others into the sense of friendship and well-being.

California in the 1970s, and young people celebrate the 'love drug'.

"I understood that our entire universe is contained in the mind and spirit. We may not choose to find access to it, we may even deny its existence, but it is indeed there inside us, and there are chemicals that can catalyse its availability."

(Alexander Shulgin, 1960, describing his first experiences with hallucinogens)

The final step

Even in the 1970s, when ecstasy was building a reputation for producing happiness and contentment, it was still mainly in the hands of professional people – doctors and therapists, for example. The drug was banned in the UK in 1977 but remained legal in the United States into the 1980s. The legal position of ecstasy concerned some people who had been involved with LSD for twenty years. Some researchers continued to believe that LSD could have remained legal, as a useful **psychological** tool, if its use had not become so widespread in the 1960s. They believed that ecstasy would suffer the same fate if it became a popular 'street drug'.

The beat goes on

In the United States, many legal manufacturers of the drug clung to the notion that they were benefiting science and society in general. They issued 'instructions' on how to take the drug, and what effects to look for. By the mid-1980s, however, their voices were lost in the loud public reaction to the drug that seemed to be taking young people by storm. Much of the reaction was not just to the drug but to the throbbing, rhythmic beat of the dance music.

Young people had realized that, in addition to making people feel good about themselves, ecstasy improved their ability to appreciate sounds, especially rhythmic sounds. It was an obvious move to cash in on this revelation by producing dance music that would energize a large group of people high on ecstasy. In 1985, the real breakthrough came when House music was developed in a Chicago club called the Warehouse (which gave the music its name). House music – and its vital ecstasy element – took the world by storm, but in that same year the US government made ecstasy illegal.

"MDMA is a tool for reaching out and touching others in soul and spirit. If responsibly used, strong bonds of unity and love can be forged that strengthen everyone involved.**"**

(From an 'instruction manual' of the Boston Group, mass manufacturers of MDMA, in the early 1980s)

Who takes ecstasy?

Many drugs are popular within a certain social group, or with those taking part in a certain activity. For many people, the path to using ecstasy lies through the world of all-night dancing at raves. Ecstasy, like amphetamines, lets people manage with less sleep (for the short term) and allows them to carry on for hours.

All night long

The link between **stimulant** drug use and all-night dancing is not exactly new. Even before the **Second World War**, people in London's West End club scene would take cocaine to stay up dancing until dawn. The rave scene – ecstasy's equivalent activity – achieves the same result. However, ecstasy adds another dimension to the previous experience, which was pursued only by a few people rather than the population as a whole.

Ecstasy has been the power behind the new dance culture because it promotes **empathy** between users. This good-time feeling contrasts strongly with the aggression that had long been associated with pubs, discos and alcohol. It also acts as a welcoming introduction to the drug for many people who would otherwise be upset by huge crowds.

Brief heyday

Use of ecstasy blossoms among people aged about sixteen, when they have achieved just about enough independence to stay out late without too much risk of punishment. It ends, often as abruptly, when people reach their twenties or even sooner. Few people in their twenties can lose a night's sleep and not suffer negative effects in their studies or work. The experience of ecstasy and raves does not usually lead people into using 'heavier' drugs so, for most people, their last 'E' tablet is also their last illegal drug.

Using ecstasy

Use of ecstasy has become much more widespread in the last decade. Its price has dropped, which is part of the reason for this spread. It also means that ecstasy need not be reserved for special occasions. As a result, ecstasy is creeping into more everyday settings and situations: one commentator suggested it is becoming a 'Tuesday night playing darts at the pub' type of drug. In other words, ecstasy is becoming an accompaniment to all sorts of activities. It is becoming harder to consider any single user as 'typical' of all who take ecstasy.

The ecstasy scene

It may be becoming harder, but it is not yet impossible to think of someone who represents the overall majority of ecstasy users. People might be attracted to ecstasy for all sorts of reasons, ranging from previous experience with **hallucinogens** and **stimulants** to simple curiosity. Those who continue to use the drug regularly do so because they identify with the ecstasy 'scene'.

Many people who use ecstasy have no idea that the extra energy it seems to provide comes at a price. The body is being slowly worn out with each sleepless night, and the way that ecstasy suppresses the appetite harms the system. As a result, ecstasy users often feel listless and burnt out during the day.

Into the night

In the early evening the ravers assemble. The night's rave might have been planned much earlier in the week, although some still occur at a moment's notice, with carloads of teenagers descending on a deserted barn or warehouse. Just before arriving at the rave, the group takes their 'E' tablets. Within an hour the effects have taken hold and the ravers begin to respond to the rhythm. The actual effects of the drug wear off after about four hours, but by that point the rave has a momentum of its own, carrying the dancers on to daybreak.

Getting sorted

In many ways, the distribution network for ecstasy is different from those for other illegal drugs. Obtaining supplies of drugs that produce a strong physical **dependence** – heroin is a good example – often means approaching unknown dealers. Many of them fit the image of the shady character offering something from the inside pocket of a raincoat.

Friendly exchanges

Getting hold of ecstasy is an altogether more informal affair. Often people buy ecstasy from people they know – close friends or people they have seen repeatedly at raves. The nearest comparison is with cannabis, which people often obtain from friends whom they trust or who might even grow it themselves. Typically, a friend or fellow raver will ask if someone is 'sorted', meaning have they got the pill they want? Very few people, however, actually make ecstasy, and that is why risks creep in, no matter who is supplying it.

A leap of faith

Because the production and sale of ecstasy is illegal its distribution operates outside any type of legal guidelines or regulations. In any transaction, the buyer cannot be sure what they are actually buying. Some ecstasy tablets have no trace of the drug in them at all, although most samples contain varying amounts of MDMA or related drugs. There is also a risk that an 'E' might contain animal tranquillizers, amphetamines, caffeine, LSD or even heroin. Drugs experts warn that ecstasy capsules are particularly risky since they can easily be opened and tampered with.

"I wouldn't touch ecstasy nowadays, not unless Doctor Alexander Shulgin himself appeared, clutching a vial of crystalline powder and saying, 'I've just synthesized a fresh batch, care to try some, m'boy?'"

(Colin Angus of The Shamen, 1995)

Wider effects

Any widespread use of an illegal drug among young people is bound to cause confusion and conflict within the family, and with non-using friends. Although some estimates suggest that more than a million young people are using ecstasy regularly – often every weekend – there are still many more who do not. Many of these people are friends of ecstasy users, and the relationship between the two groups of young people is mirrored by reactions within families.

Mixture of emotions

Most parents of people who take ecstasy were in their late teens – the peak ecstasy period – about thirty years ago. The late 1960s was a time of intense drug use, coupled with parental conflict and a general sense of rebellion against traditional values. It comes as something of a surprise for many parents – even those with 'drug histories' that might include LSD and amphetamines – to face the same behaviour in their own children that their parents faced in themselves.

Apart from the issue of staying out late, the dance scene in itself does not prove to be a terrible threat to family life. Parents know that they must separate their disapproval of drug use from other feelings about raves themselves. A survey carried out in August 1997 by the British drug awareness organization Release, for example, showed that drugs were far from being the main attraction of raves. Instead, most young people said that they were more interested in the music, socializing, the atmosphere and the dancing. Drugs came fifth on the list, while looking for a sexual partner – another area of parental concern – hardly got a mention.

❝Parents are often angry, because it's easier to be angry when showing your concern than being calm. Before anything can be done about drugs, people have to understand their relationships.❞

(Phil Harris of the Bristol Drugs Project)

Wider effects

A test of friendship

Unless the drug-use question becomes highly charged, most ecstasy users themselves feel that family relationships are not threatened. For their part, they do not expect their parents to take – or even know much about – ecstasy. The **empathy** that is a feature of ecstasy might even help relations.

Friendships, however, are a different matter. The gulf between an ecstasy-taking teenager and their parents is to be expected. The gulf between ecstasy users and non-users is harder to bridge. Taking any drug regularly puts a strain on friendships with people who do not partake. First, there is the problem of one being 'cool' and the other being behind the times. The non-user often feels left out when Monday morning conversations at school turn to ecstasy experiences over the previous weekend. Second, a change of attitude can take place in the ecstasy user. Ecstasy makes it hard to take many things seriously, and studying hard or training regularly at sports – even if these were once part of someone's major interests – might seem a little pointless.

Paying out

Supply of ecstasy has managed to keep up with – and even overtake – the growing demand for the drug. In real terms, or the fraction of available spending money that it costs, ecstasy has fallen in price since it became a popular drug. In some areas it has dropped to as little as £8 a tablet for bulk purchases, or £10–15 for a single tablet.

Many people can get the sense of shared experience – and 'feel good' buzz – through activities in which drugs play no part.

"The price has dropped to £8 a tab…Ten years ago when we first started seeing it, it was tied up with the ritual of raving. It was £25 and the price preserved the ritual, it was special. Now it's a more normal drug."

(Mike Linnell of Manchester's Lifeline organization)

Life with ecstasy

Using ecstasy involves running risks that many ravers choose to ignore or to play down. These risks are not just confined to regular users; even a single ecstasy tablet (see panel on pages 31–32) can lead to death. While it is very uncertain whether anybody has died directly from the **toxic** effects of the drug, fatalities have occurred in three other categories.

Overheating (far right) is a common problem among ecstasy users. Users with even minor heart conditions can face risks usually associated with older patients (below).

Heat-stroke

Most ecstasy deaths – averaging about seven per year in Britain during the 1990s – fall in this category, which results from overheating. Ecstasy raises the body temperature and encourages repeated behaviour (like frantic dancing) which also raises temperatures. Added to this is the hot environment of most dance floors. Body temperature can exceed the danger limit of 40°C. Symptoms then include **convulsions**, very low blood pressure and highly increased heart rate. MDMA seems to interfere with the way blood **coagulates** in the body. If it coagulates in the lungs, the person dies of suffocation.

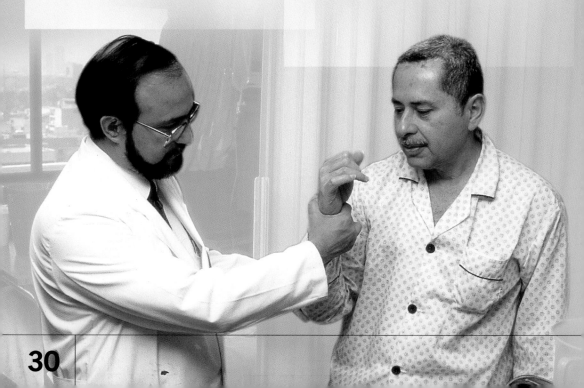

Too much fluid

Most ravers realize that they need to replace the fluids they lose through sweating and increased body temperature. Drinking too much, however, can lead to trouble. Again, the problem seems to relate to signals that MDMA sends within the body. It causes the kidneys to fail in their efforts to expel excess fluids from the body. Water is retained in the body, especially in brain cells that regulate bodily functions such as breathing and heart rate. Symptoms include dizziness and confusion. If it is serious, the person falls into a **coma**.

Heart failure

The third major cause of ecstasy-related death comes from the rise in heart rate and blood pressure during an ecstasy high. Although most young people are fit enough to cope with this increased pressure on the circulatory system, others might have even minor heart conditions that had previously been unnoticed. Faced with such a sudden rise, a faulty **coronary** system might fail, causing death.

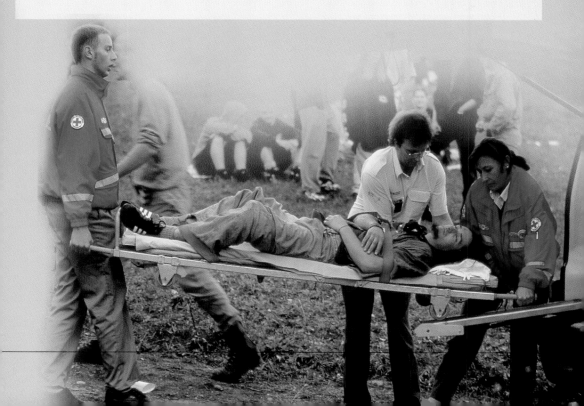

Life with ecstasy

The case of Leah Betts

One of the most tragic and well-publicized stories in the history of ecstasy use centres on Leah Betts. On 11 November 1995 Leah and her friends were celebrating her eighteenth birthday with a special party at her home. Among the guests were Leah's father Paul, who was a former police officer, and her stepmother Jan, a community school nurse. Just before the party, at about 7.45pm, Leah took an ecstasy tablet – it was the fourth or fifth time that she had taken an 'E'.

At about 12.45am, Leah began to feel hot and uncomfortable and within minutes she was retching violently in the washbasin of her parents' bathroom. Her head throbbed with pain and she was screaming, 'Please help me!' Leah stopped breathing just fifteen minutes after she began to feel ill. She was rushed to hospital, where she spent four days on a breathing machine. It was believed that Leah was in a **coma**, but in fact she had died from 'Brain Stem Death' when she had stopped breathing on the night of the party.

The breathing machine was turned off on 16 November, by which time her story was known across Britain and the world. Some pro-ecstasy supporters tried to argue that she had taken a 'doctored' pill, but the medical records indicate that the tablet had been pure MDMA, and her cause of death was listed as 'ecstasy poisoning'. In fact, no one has yet died from a 'doctored' pill – all ecstasy deaths so far have been linked to pure MDMA.

Posters showing Leah's face, on which was superimposed the word 'Sorted', were used for some time to raise awareness about the dangers of ecstasy.

❝Leah always told her mother and father she was appalled by drugs. But perhaps, like so many youngsters, she did not see Ecstasy as a drug at all.❞

(*The Sunday Times*, writing about the death of Leah Betts, 1995)

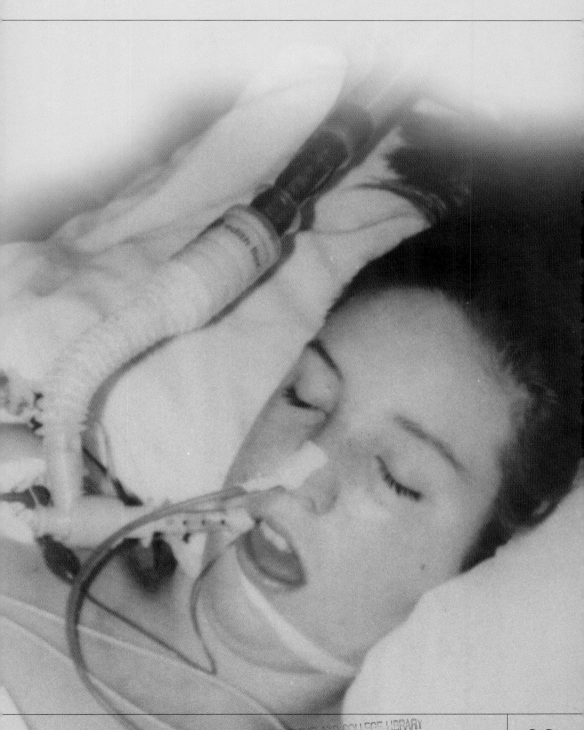

Rave risks

Although ecstasy does not score highly in terms of **dependence**, repeated use can lead to a range of problems – some minor and others more serious. People do build up **tolerance**, and the higher dose that they end up taking can open them up to some **toxic** side-effects. Among these are nausea, dizziness, jaw tension and – most importantly – **heat-stroke**.

The heat is on

Although ecstasy is nearly a century old, it has only been a 'headline' drug for about a decade. It may be too soon to tell how many medical complications might arise from repeated use of the drug, although researchers are beginning to gather evidence that it might cause long-term liver damage in some people.

The issue that has caught the public imagination (and which is dealt with more fully on pages 31–32) is the problem of overheating and heat-stroke. Both of these problems can arise in a first-time experience, but they are more likely to occur when someone has been taking relatively high doses over a long time. Basically, ecstasy is a **stimulant**, it makes users able to dance longer, which in turn makes them hot.

The drug also raises the body temperature, which makes the user hotter still. These two factors, coupled with the hot and crowded conditions on most dance floors, mean that pints of water are sweated out. The result can lead to **dehydration** and heat-stroke.

Other concerns

The basic principle of tolerance increases the problem of overheating and is also linked to other negative side-effects. Here, the research becomes even more complicated and sometimes **contradictory**, but concerns have definitely been raised. For example, four Scottish ravers died in 1992 of **brain haemorrhages**, although three of them had also been using amphetamines. Equally troubling is the suggestion that ecstasy might damage brain cells. The danger here is that the drug damages those cells that produce and transmit a chemical 'messenger' known as serotonin. Since knowledge about serotonin itself is limited – it may control sleep, appetite and mood – it becomes even harder to say with certainty just what harm ecstasy might do.

The ecstasy industry

Ecstasy has evolved from being a 'way station' drug, used in the preparation of other drugs, to become a popular drug in its own right. Despite its illegal status in nearly every country, it continues to be produced in vast quantities. Some of the production is thanks to the many chemical **formulae** that Alexander Shulgin and other chemists have put in the public domain over the years – virtual step-by-step instructions on how to produce ecstasy and other **derivatives** of its parent drug, MDA.

Return to research

Even if ecstasy is nowhere near as powerful as LSD, their history and the industry surrounding them have run parallel (see pages 14–17). Many of the same voices that argued – while ecstasy was still legal in the United States – for a pause before letting it go public are now pressing for further research.

News reporters must sift through rumour, hearsay and conflicting medical reports to try to present a clear picture of ecstasy to their readers.

Ecstasy was banned in 1985 in the United States specifically because of the fears that it would damage brain cells (see page 34). At the time, the evidence leading to this conclusion was based on animal experiments. Moreover, the main experiments conducted by Doctor George Ricaurte in Baltimore used much higher doses of MDMA than those taken by humans. The drug was **injected** into rats and monkeys, rather than being taken orally, which is the way most ecstasy users take it.

❝I think it is important to recognize that, particularly in the rave situation, there are individuals taking six, eight or ten tablets over a twenty-four to forty-eight hour period. So some of the more recent patterns of human MDMA use in the rave setting are beginning to mimic the regimen of drug administration that we employed in our monkeys.❞

(Doctor George Ricaurte, defending his 1980s animal research on MDMA)

The ecstasy industry

The unknown purpose of serotonin (see page 34) in the brain has meant that Ricaurte's findings – that ecstasy *could* cause brain damage – are not the last word in the ecstasy industry. One big question mark has remained – just how *does* it affect humans? The beginnings of an answer emerged in California in May 1994, when Doctor Charles Grobb became the first doctor legally to give ecstasy to a human being since its **criminalization**. Grobb's findings were far from earth-shattering but they confirmed several points that had been observed on dance floors. First, ecstasy does cause an increase in core temperature in the body, even in the people tested who remained in bed throughout the period. Second, there is a mild but persistent raising of blood pressure.

Both of these findings fit in with what is described as **anecdotal** research – the first-hand accounts of those who take the drug. They also highlight the dangers of overheating (tied in with temperature rise) and heart-related problems (with increased blood pressure). What none of the search has discovered, however, is just how ecstasy produces its unique sense of **empathy** among those who take it.

Dutch practicalities

These American researchers, and others doing work on ecstasy, stress that their work is done with pure MDMA. What people actually buy on the street or in clubs is a different matter, since it can easily be mixed with other drugs. The Dutch have become particularly concerned by the risk associated with 'doctored' ecstasy. They note that there are two types of ecstasy being sold on the street. The first is actually MDMA, but is very closely linked to the powerful MDA. The second is entirely fake, comprising aspirin, amphetamines, LSD or other drugs.

To check on the purity of ecstasy being sold, the Dutch use fourteen testing centres, where 'street ecstasy' is taken for analysis in laboratories run by the Dance Drugs Project in Amsterdam. Any worrying findings (to do with powerful or dangerous additives) are posted on the doors of Dutch nightclubs in time for the next weekend's peak ecstasy use.

Seemingly identical, a selection of ecstasy tablets can easily contain a number of 'doctored' doses.

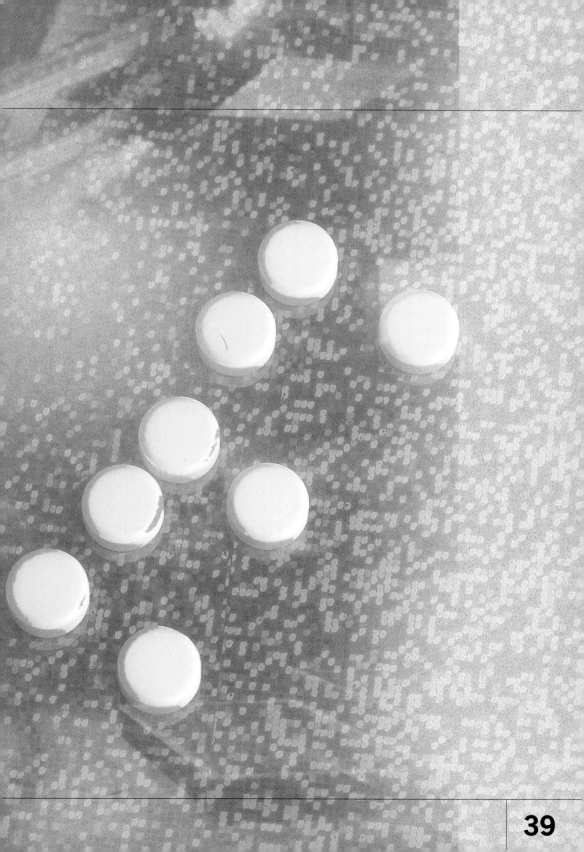

Cashing in

While researchers have been occupied in trying to get to the truth about ecstasy and its effects, the drug itself has continued to enjoy widespread popularity. As a result, the ecstasy scene, sometimes described as 'E culture', generates huge amounts of money. Some of this money finds its way into the hands of drug dealers and **traffickers**, but ecstasy trafficking does not have the same sense of international intrigue, profits and violence that accompanies the trade in heroin or cocaine.

Traditional trips

There is, however, a vast area of economic activity that has benefited directly from the whole club culture. The late 1990s saw a move away from the massive, unplanned raves in abandoned warehouses and towards more commercial clubs. Entrance fees of £10 a head can still generate a good profit for a nightclub even if it knows that sales of alcohol are unlikely to be very high (see panel).

Tourism is another area of buzzing economic activity. The Balearic Islands, off the Mediterranean coast of Spain, have traditionally been linked to the dance culture. Balearic music, allegedly heard by two London DJs while on holiday there, acted as a balance to the harder-edged sounds of House music in the clubs of the 1980s. One of the smallest of the Balearic group, Ibiza, has been in the forefront of the rave scene since that period. Thousands of foreign visitors land there each summer, simply to sample the club scene. The island, which has always had its share of foreign income, has received a further boost from this band of clubbers.

Threat to the drinks industry?

One of the curious economic side-effects about increased ecstasy use has been the decline in alcohol-drinking among clubbers and others who take ecstasy regularly. At many raves the only visible drinks are either mineral water or soft drinks, which ravers consume to counteract the threat of overheating. The cost of an ecstasy high, compared with the cost of alcohol, is another threat to the alcohol industry. In 1992, Richard Carr, a senior executive in the huge British drinks company Allied-Tetley-Lyons, said, 'Youngsters can get ecstasy for £10 or £12 and get a much better buzz than they can from alcohol. It is a major threat to alcohol-led business.'

Cashing in

The music industry has also benefited. Memories of summer holidays in Ibiza, in turn, have led to annual compilations, which are advertised aggressively each year. The 'summer sounds' of Ibiza return to London, Manchester, Frankfurt and Amsterdam, providing a soundtrack for another winter's dancing in clubs, which in turn gets people ready for the next year's 'new sound'.

Seeping into society

The whole culture surrounding the dance scene, with which ecstasy is so closely linked, has led to many developments in the wider world of business. Companies with no obvious link to drug-taking generally – or ecstasy in particular – have seen the potential for generating more sales among the young. Products such as soft drinks, convenience foods and even banking services are advertised in a way that reminds ecstasy users of the wacky point of view that the drug produces. These same products have been 'rebranded', in some cases, to be brighter and more carefree in their design.

One major Australian **brewer** even supplied blank cassette labels with purchases of its beer. The unspoken purpose of the labels was to help 'bedroom producers' – individuals compiling their own dance compilations at home. The strategy – although perfectly legal – was to identify the company with the whole dance culture and to emphasize its special appeal to young people.

❝The House movement has been herded into a capitalist kraal. Club culture used to talk a lot about 'freedom'. It's turning out to be the freedom to be farmed.❞

(Journalist Stephen Kingston, quoted in *Altered State* about the 'business boom' in rave culture)

Legal matters

The legal position on ecstasy is straightforward – it is illegal in nearly every country where it is consumed. The UK was one of the first countries to ban MDMA. The move came in 1977 after an illegal laboratory was raided in the Midlands. Police found that the chemist had prepared a **hallucinogenic** amphetamine that was not yet illegal, and that he had **formulae** for other drugs of this type, including what is now known as ecstasy. The British authorities decided to stay one jump ahead of such **underground** chemists by introducing an amendment to the Misuse of Drugs Act 1971. The amendment was designed to control all amphetamine-like **compounds** including MDMA.

In Britain, MDMA is also in Schedule 1 of the relations that prohibit doctors from **prescribing** it and it is a Designated Drug, which means that researchers can only use the drug after obtaining a licence from the Home Office.

The ban in the United States, which took effect in May 1985, places MDMA under Schedule 1 of US drug laws. This classification means that nobody can legally manufacture, sell or use ecstasy for any purposes.

In Australia it is illegal to use, possess, produce or supply ecstasy. Penalties range from a $2000 fine and/or 2 years in prison to a $500,000 fine and/or life imprisonment. It is also illegal to drive under the influence of any drug.

The Misuse of Drugs Act

As the old saying goes, ignorance is no defence in a court of law. In the case of ecstasy and most controlled drugs, the law in question is the Misuse of Drugs Act 1971, which divides drugs into three classes and gives guidelines for penalties. Class A drugs, which include cocaine, crack, heroin and LSD, are considered most serious and the penalty for supply can be life imprisonment. Since 1977, ecstasy has also been part of this classification. The maximum sentence for possession is up to seven years' imprisonment plus a fine. For **trafficking** offences – including the supply or intent to supply – the maximum sentence can be life imprisonment. Ecstasy is now the most seized Class A drug in most British police force areas.

Organisers of many public events mount
their own drugs checks to make sure no one
with drugs is admitted.

45

Treatment and counselling

When people talk about treatment and counselling, they are usually referring to the large group of drugs that lead to **dependence**, especially physical dependence. Some form of outside help – in the form of therapy sessions, substitute drugs or one-on-one counselling – is often necessary to overcome the compulsive desire to have more of the drug. Ecstasy is different. Although repeated exposure to the rave setting might make people more inclined to become regular users – because the 'normal world' seems increasingly dull – the problem does not lie in the area of dependence. Instead, awareness of the risks of ecstasy (see pages 30–35) is the key to remaining healthy and making an informed choice about whether the pleasures of the ecstasy high outweigh dangers that might prove fatal.

Coping with trouble

The best course of action at a rave, of course, is not to take any drugs. However, since ecstasy is so common, especially in these settings, it is important to know exactly how to help someone who is in trouble. Most of the following points are common sense, but when people are high they often lose the ability to look after themselves.

- Make sure they have regular intakes of drinks such as water and fruit juices – about a pint an hour, but no more. Don't let them drink alcohol – it **dehydrates** the body further.

- Do not let them dance for long stretches of time and make sure they take time out regularly.

- See that they are wearing loose clothing to let the body cool itself more easily.

- Don't let them be tempted to take a higher dose to repeat the experience of that first high. Increased doses of ecstasy also increase the risks involved.

Treatment and counselling

Dehydration alert

Remember that a failure to sweat, cramps, dizziness and nausea are all signs that there is an immediate risk of **dehydration**. If you see a friend dehydrating, remember to get help immediately, either from a **paramedic** if there is one present, or by dialling for an ambulance. Get the person somewhere cool – outside if possible – and splash them with cold water.

Raving at Glastonbury

Each June many thousands of people converge on a farm near Glastonbury, a lovely setting in the south-west of England. They come for the music, and there are acts ranging from mainstream rock to folk, world music and rap. Recent festivals have seen the introduction of a special 'dance tent', where techno-beat, Balearic and House music provide a rave atmosphere.

The owner of the farm, Michael Eavis, has long experience in dealing with young people, music – and drugs. 'When young people are gathered together one will always find drugs,' he notes. 'We have 100,000 (mostly young) people attending our festival and we certainly acknowledge that drugs are being used and experimented with over this time.'

Eavis makes the point that you don't need drugs to appreciate the music – the 'buzz' of the crowd should be enough stimulation. He also cites another good reason for steering clear of drugs in this setting: 'It is very large, very exciting but very bewildering and strange for someone experimenting with drugs. Don't do it – you could certainly ruin your festival – if not more.'

Glastonbury, recognizing that even this advice might not be enough, takes precautions appropriate to specific types of drug use. 'In the dance tent, for example, we have medics and people constantly giving out water.' For those who have unpleasant **psychological** side-effects, either from LSD or ecstasy, 'we have a psychiatrist on site and a large team of welfare services to comfort, support and care for distressed young people.'

It should be noted that in many ways, Glastonbury is unusual in its two-pronged approach – increasing awareness and on-site emergency provision. At most raves, the people have to rely on themselves or the good sense of those around them.

Public health publications like this poster help young people get the full picture about ecstasy and its many side-effects.

ecstasy
know the score

Take E now and you might feel fine. But if you take E you're a human guinea-pig because no-one knows what the long term effects are. Unlike other pills you can buy, E hasn't been medically tested.

What we do know about E is that some people have suffered from strokes, depression, mental illness and even fallen into comas.

There's also some indication that taking E might lead to brain damage. Nobody can be 100% sure, but it's some gamble for a night out.

You sweat a lot when you dance, so it's not just the water you've got to replace, there's sodium too. Fruit juice or an energy drink should do the job. It works for marathon runners.

There's some confusion about how much water to drink on E. When dancing, you need to sip about a pint of non-alcoholic liquid an hour to replace lost fluids. Also remember to wear loose, light clothes and just chill out regularly.

If you'd like more information about drugs or just a talk, give us a call free and in total confidence.

People to talk to

Ecstasy has swept into the newspapers and public eye generally because of its rapid rise in popularity. Although it has become incredibly popular with a certain segment of society, the overall effects of the drug remain unknown. At the same time, it has a reputation as a 'happy drug' that draws people together. As a result, many young people might be tempted, either by these examples or by friends, to try 'E'. This type of **peer pressure** is not helpful, but it is a strong and persuasive force.

Other voices

There are people who can put things in a different perspective, either by giving first-hand accounts of their own drug experiences or by outlining the clear dangers of what is known about the risks associated with ecstasy. Parents and older family members are usually the best people to turn to first.

A school setting can provide an informative – but informal – opportunity to share knowledge about ecstasy.

Unfortunately, the teenage years are often the period when young people feel that they have least in common with their parents. With a drug like ecstasy, this gulf seems even wider. Even sympathetic teachers and others in authority locally might seem too close to home.

The UK has a wide range of telephone contacts – many of them free of charge and most of them anonymous – where young people can find out more about ecstasy and other drugs. Many of the organizations listed in the Information and advice section (pages 52–53) are specialist phone lines. They provide such a telephone service, or they can suggest local agencies throughout the UK. Others are geared specifically to queries coming from younger people. Whether you approach one of these organizations, or a family member, a youth leader or teacher, the important thing is to be able to talk – and listen – freely about your drug concerns. Sharing a problem or worry is the first step to solving it.

Information and advice

The UK is well served by organizations providing advice, counselling and other information relating to drug use. All of the contacts listed on these pages are helpful springboards for obtaining such advice or for providing confidential information over the telephone or by post.

Drug awareness contacts

ADFAM NATIONAL
Tel: 020 7928 8900
This is a national (UK) hotline for the friends and families of drug users. It provides confidential support and information to anyone who is worried about someone close to them who is using drugs.

British Association for Counselling (BAC)
1 Regent Place, Rugby CV21 2PJ
www.bac.co.uk
The BAC has an extensive directory of counselling services relating to drugs and other issues throughout the UK. Enquiries are by post only. Enclose an SAE for a list of counsellors in your area.

ISDD (Institute for the Study of Drug Dependence), Waterbridge House, 32–36 Loman Street, London SE1 0EE
Tel: 020 7928 1211 www.isdd.co.uk
The ISDD has the largest drugs reference library in Europe and provides leaflets and other publications. SCODA (the Standing Committee on Drug Abuse) is located at the same address (tel: 020 7928 9500) and is one of the best UK contacts for information on drugs.

Narcotics Anonymous
UK Service Office, PO Box 198J
London N19 3LS, Tel: 020 7498 9904
www.ukna.org
Narcotics Anonymous (NA) is a network of self-help groups tackling the problem of drug dependence on the same lines as Alcoholics Anonymous.

National Drugs Helpline
Tel: 0800 776600
The Helpline provides a free telephone contact for all aspects of drug use and has a database covering all of the British Isles for further information about specific drugs or regional information.

Release
Tel: 020 7603 8654
www.release.org.uk
Release operates a 24-hour helpline which provides advice on drug use and legal issues surrounding the subject.

Youth Access
1A Taylors Yard, 67 Alderbrook Road, London SW12 8AD, Tel: 020 8772 9900
Youth Access is an organization which refers young people to their local counselling service. It has a database of approximately 350 such services throughout the UK.

Contacts in the United States

Child Welfare League of America
440 First Street N.W., Washington, DC 20001, Tel: 202/638–2952
www.cwla.org
The Child Welfare League of America, based in Washington, provides useful contacts across the country in most areas relating to young people's problems, many of them related to drug involvement.

DARE America
PO Box 775, Dumfries, VA 22026
Tel: 703/860–3273
www.dare-america.com
Drug Abuse Resistance and Education (DARE) America is a national organization that links law-enforcement and educational resources to provide up-to-date and comprehensive information about all aspects of drug use.

Youth Power
300 Lakeside Drive, Oakland, CA
94612, Tel: 510/451–6666, ext. 24
Youth Power is a nationwide organization involved in widening awareness of drug-related problems. It sponsors clubs and local affiliates across the country in an effort to help young people make their own sensible choices about drugs, and to work against the negative effects of peer pressure.

Contacts in Australia

ADCA
PO Box 269, Woden, ACT 2606
www.adca.org.au
The Alcohol and other Drug Council of Australia (ADCA), based in the Capital Territory, gives an overview of drug awareness organizations in Australia. Most of their work is carried out over the Internet but the postal address provides a useful link for those who are not on-line.

Australian Drug Foundation
409 King Street, West Melbourne,
VIC 3003, Tel: 03 9278 8100
www.adf.org.au
The Australian Drug Foundation (ADF) has a wide range of information on all aspects of drugs, their effects and the legal position in Australia. It also provides handy links to state- and local-based drug organizations.

Centre for Education and Information on Drugs and Alcohol
Private Mail Bag 6, Rozelle, NSW 2039
Tel: 02 9818 0401   www.ceida.net.au
The Centre for Education and Information on Drugs and Alcohol is the ideal contact for information on drug programmes throughout Australia. It also has one of the most extensive libraries on drug-related subjects in the world.

Further reading

Buzzed, by Cynthia Kuhn, Scott Swartzwelder and Wilkie Wilson; New York and London: W.W. Norton and Company, 1998

Drugs, by Anita Naik, part of Wise Guides Series; London: Hodder Children's Books, 1997

Drugs and the Party Line, by Kevin Williamson; London: Rebel Inc., 1997

Drugs: The Facts, HEA leaflet; London: Health Education Authority, 1997

Drugs Wise, by Melanie McFadyean; Cambridge: Icon books, 1997

A Parent's Guide to Drugs and Alcohol, HEA leaflet; London: Health Education Authority, 1998

Street Drugs, by Andrew Tyler; London: Coronet, 3rd edition, 1995

Taking Drugs Seriously, A Parent's Guide to Young People's Drug Use, by Julian Cohen and James Kay; London: Thorsons, 1994

The Score: Facts about Drugs, HEA leaflet; London: Health Education Authority, 1998

Glossary

addictive
leading to dependence

anecdotal
relying on word of mouth

brain haemorrhage
a bursting of a blood vessel in the brain

brewer
a company that produces beer

catalyze
to cause something to develop

coagulate
to turn from a liquid into a solid

Cold War
the period lasting roughly 45 years after the Second World War when the United States and its capitalist Western allies competed with the Soviet Union and its communist allies for world influence

coma
a state of prolonged unconsciousness when a person does not respond to sights or sounds

compound
a chemical combination of things

contradictory
offering two opposing conclusions

convulsion
uncontrolled shaking of the body

coronary
the heart and blood circulation

criminalization
being made illegal

dehydrate/dehydration
to lose essential fluids

dependence
the physical or psychological craving for something

derivative
a drug or other substance that has been produced from a different original source

empathy
a kind understanding of how others feel

euphoria
a sense that everything is wonderful

First World War
the war (1914–1918) between Germany, Austria and their allies against Britain, France and their allies

formulae
chemical codes for producing substances

hallucinogens
a substance that produces hallucinations (seeing things which are not really there)

heat-stroke
possible suffocation because of overheating of the body

injected
pumped into the body, usually with a type of needle and syringe

intelligence
the government department dealing with spying and information about possible enemies

kraal
Afrikaans word meaning a closed-in area

overdose
a dose of a drug that is too much for the body to absorb or cope with

paramedic
someone with expert first-aid training

patent
to gain the legal right to be the only person or company to produce something for sale

peer pressure
the pressure from friends of the same age to behave in a certain way

pharmaceutical
the medical use of chemical sciences

pharmacologist
a chemist who studies the production of medicines

prescribe
to give (by a doctor) a document requesting supply of a certain medicine

psychological
relating to the mind and behaviour

regimen
a set routine in an experiment

respiratory
relating to the lungs or breathing

Second World War
the war (1939–1945) between Germany, Japan and their allies against Britain, the United States and their allies

stimulant
a drug that makes people more alert or energetic

suppressant
something that decreases a desire

synthesize
to produce by chemical processes

synthetic
produced by chemical processes

therapeutic
medically useful

tolerance
the way in which the body learns to accept or expect more of a substance

toxic
poisonous to the body

trafficker
someone who deals with the distribution of drugs, often across international borders

underground
away from view of the police or other law-enforcement groups

withdrawal
negative physical effects of giving up a substance

Index